ES 1

Beach Party

by

George Weston

BLUEBELL PRESS

First published 1986

Illustrated by Linda Knight

BLUEBELL PRESS

Published by Bluebell Press Ltd,
Shelley House, 38 Shelley Road, Preston,
Lancashire, England PR2 2DB

ISBN 0 948440 52 X

Introduction

Just over a thousand years ago, the Vikings landed on the Isle of Man.

Two small dolls travelled with them on their long journey—Viktor the Viking and Millie Any Um.

Soon forgotton, the dolls were left by the Viking children. After a terrible storm they were buried deep in the sand.

Many years passed by and grass grew over the sand leaving no trace of our little friends.

But strange and wonderful things do happen. Read on to discover the magical story.

Welcome to the island of the Manx Men!

It was a hot, sunny day in Shallbe—just right for the beach party. Peel Pete had put up posters all over Shallbe, inviting the Manxmen.

The notice read: "Bring your own potato, a prize will be awarded for the best fancy dress, starts twelve o'clock till late."

The twins asked Major Ramsey if they could stay up late for the party. As usual, the Major said yes.

Viktor had received his first letter in Shallbe and was very excited. He opened the envelope and took out a map which had a large cross on it. What did it mean? Who was it from?

Poor Viktor. His first letter and he didn't know who had sent it.

The sun is hot, the sky is blue
We're having a party, there's lots to do

The twins were jumping with delight
They could stay up late tonight

Viktor receives a map with a cross
Which leaves the poor chap at a loss

The shops were busy in town. All the Manxmen were trying on their outfits for the beach party. The fruit shop had quickly sold all the potatoes for the big supper that evening.

Laxey Lil was trying on a new pair of boots in the boutique, when she met Castletown Kate.

"Oh, I wish I could dress like you," Kate said to Lil.

"I know what we'll do," said Lil excitedly, "we'll change clothes for the party. No one will be able to tell the difference."

"Oh yes," cried Kate, "I would love that."

What nobody knew was that all the Manxmen had changed their clothes. All, that is, except T T Tommy. But who had changed with who?

Manxmen mingled, shops were busy
With all the rush, they all felt dizzy

They tried on outfits large and small
It's party time for one and all

All changed clothes, both old and new
But I wonder who changed clothes with who

Viktor arrived with Millie, or was it Pete with Fairy Fran? Rocky and Larry were next, but it could well have been Larry and Rocky. The two Onchan Eddies arrived, as if one wasn't enough! Then came Kate and Lil. Even the twins had swapped clothes.

Major Ramsey, who was Douglas Douggie, was a little surprised when he saw his little Manxman grandson playing with a doll.

And so the party began. Everyone had their baked potato for tea. As usual, the fairies toasted marshmallows and drank hot chocolate.

''Let's play some games,'' said one of the Onchan Eddies.

''No,'' said Sam Snaefell, ''let's build the biggest sandcastle in the world.''

Was it Pete or was it Millie
Everyone looked rather silly

No one knew who was who
Of Onchan Eddie, there were two

Baked potatoes were had for tea
And a great big sandcastle built by the sea

Now while the party was going on, Connie Cone was selling her ice creams. They were only five pence each and the queue stretched for miles. However, as usual, Onchan Eddie had other ideas.

He set up his own ice cream stand. Poor Connie. All the Manxmen children went to buy Eddie's ice cream because his was a penny cheaper.

By now, everyone knew who the real Onchan Eddie was.

The sand castle was getting bigger and bigger. In fact, it was so high, Sam Snaefell had to climb to the top to put the Shallbe flag in position.

Connie Cone was selling ice cream
The party was going like a dream

Onchan Eddie hatched a plot
His ices were cheaper, he sold a lot

Sam, he climbed the great sandcastle
And reached the top without any hassle

Viktor thought that every castle should have a moat and some tunnels, so he immediately set to work.

Millie helped the fairies cook some magical food from the book of spells. The twins were busy burying Grandad Ramsey up to his neck in the sand, throwing doughnuts on to his moustache.

What a party it was turning out to be.

''Come and dance,'' shouted Elastic Edd. So they cleared some of the sand away and made a dance floor. No one knew who they were dancing with and what's more they didn't even care.

As there were no donkeys to ride on Shallbe, T T Tommy gave Glide-By rides instead.

Moats and tunnels are a must
As Viktor digs, there's a cloud of dust

Magical food from the book of spells
Stop throwing doughnuts, the Major yells

Come and dance shouts Elastic Eddie
Hurry up, the dance floors ready

Viktor's tunnel was getting longer and longer. After a short while he came up through the sand right under Eddie's ice cream stand. Suddenly, the sand began to give way. Eddie and his cheap ice cream started to sink into the long tunnel that Viktor had built.

What a sight. Two hands, tightly holding two cornets, gradually disappeared down the hole.

Poor Eddie, will he ever learn?

This put Connie back in business and everyone was happy.

However, Eddie was not giving up. He scrambled out of the hole and went away to think of another crafty scheme.

T T Tommy was doing a roaring trade. He was giving free rides in Glide-By up and down the beach.

But where was Rocky while all this was going on?

Eddie's sales were getting stronger
While Viktor's tunnel got much longer

Now Eddie gets that sinking feeling
To put an end to all his dealing

Round the beach Glide-By goes
But where is Larry? No-one knows

"Balloons: red, yellow, blue and green; the cheapest balloons you've ever seen." Yes, Eddie was up to his tricks again! There he was with a big bunch of balloons, selling them for ten pence each. He didn't have many buyers.

Peel Pete was invited to open the sand castle. It was named Castletown. This pleased Kate. She had the castle named after her, even if it was only for one day.

Major Ramsey was still buried up to his neck in sand. He could hardly be seen for all the doughnuts covering his face. The twins had enjoyed themselves playing their new game.

It would not be long before the tide came in. Everyone went to inspect the castle only to find Larry (dressed as Rocky) lying flat in the sand. The salt had got to his batteries again. A quick spell from Fairy Fran soon put Larry back on his feet.

Balloons: red, yellow, blue and green
the cheapest balloons you've ever seen

As all the Manxmen gathered round
Pete named the castle, Castletown

Fairy Fran had cast her spell
And so their day had ended well

"Look . . . Look . . ." cried Millie, as she pointed to the sky, "there's Eddie."

He was holding so many balloons that the wind had lifted him up and was blowing him back to Shallbe Castle.

It was getting dark. Everything was packed away as the fire died down. The tide came in. Just as quickly as the Manxmen had built the sand castle, the water carried it away into the sea.

Another day ended on the magical island. But what about Viktor's map? Where exactly was that cross?

To follow the further exciting adventures of
Viktor and Millie, and meet more of the
Manxmen, read Book 6–A Major Find.

The
Manxmen
The Manxmen Are Coming
by
George
Weston
No. 1

The
Manxmen
Magical Mystery Trip
No. 2

The
Manxmen
Peel Pete's
by
No. 3

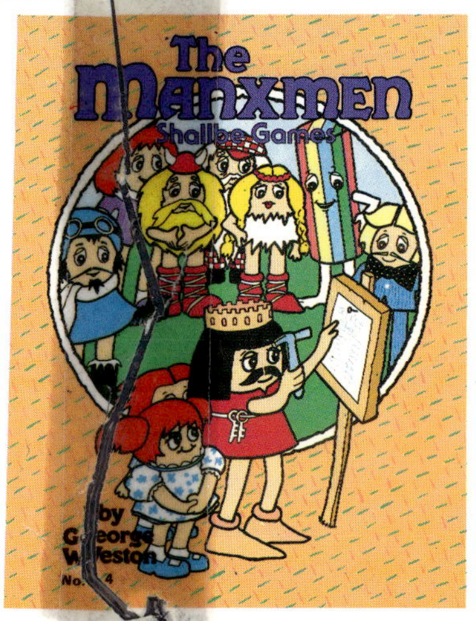
The
Manxmen
Shallbe Games
by

The
Manxmen
Beach Party
FANCY DRESS
PARTY
Bring your own potato!
A prize will be awarded
for the best fancy dress.
by
George
Weston
No. 5

The
Manxmen
A Major Find
by
George
Weston
No. 6

We hope you have enjoyed reading about the Manxmen.
You can follow their further adventures in the first six serials listed below.

1. The Manxmen Are Coming.
2. Magical Mystery Trip.
3. Peel Pete's Cannon.
4. Shallbe Games.
5. Beach Party.
6. A Major Find.